GO DO

AROUND

Cle Elum

A Guide To Year-Round Recreational Opportunities
In Central Washington State's Upper Kittitas County

By Carla Black and Angel Rodriguez

Published by
Frontier Publishing
Seattle, WA 98109
for Evergreen Books

Cover Design by Tracy Noot

If you would like to have a book, like this
one, about your community contact:

Evergreen Books
1314 N.E. 56th Street
Seattle, WA 98105

ISBN 0-939116-30-8

TABLE of CONTENTS

Introduction

Whatever you like to do, Cle Elum and Upper Kittitas County is the place to do it. From hiking, to bicycling, to skiing, to just sitting and reading a book, come do it in Cle Elum. The sun is probably shining. And if you like it hot in the summer, it is hotter; if you like it cold in the winter, it's colder; and if you like it dry all the time, it's dryer! (Than west of the Cascades, that is.)

We discovered the wonderful woodlands of Upper Kittitas County when we were working on our *Guide to Mountain Bike Riding in Washington* a few years ago. Like many travelers on I-90, we had passed Cle Elum hundreds of times, only stopping for a meal occasionally. It wasn't until we had the task of exploring the Cascades that we stopped for a good look around Cle Elum. What a treasure chest! The Alpine Lakes Wilderness to the north, miles of trail open for bicycling and motorcycling to the south, and beautiful country roads in the valley. Then add some of the best snowmobiling in the state, and fine fishing in the Yakima River, and you have an unexplored paradise.

It is only 90 minutes from Seattle via I-90 - an easy drive any time of year. And it only takes a half an hour longer from Everett or Tacoma.

We have just scratched the surface of places to enjoy the outdoors in Upper Kittitas County. We highlight the best and the most accessible outdoor recreation opportunities. In the opening to each section we have listed other sources of information, so you can come back and explore some more.

A Wenatchee National Forest Visitor's Map is useful no matter what you're going to do on Forest lands. You can buy one at the Cle Elum Ranger District Office for $3.00. The Ranger District Office also has information on more places to go hiking, mountain biking, snowmobiling, and where to enjoy other outdoor activities on National Forest land. To get to the office: go west on 2nd St. in Cle Elum, and they are just past the city park on the left. Their hours are 7:45 am to 4:30 pm weekdays, and 7:30 am to 4:00 pm (closed for lunch) Saturdays. Call (509) 674-4411 to check on

Sunday hours, or on anything else related to the Wenatchee National Forest. Maps are also available at the Snoqualmie National Forest office in downtown Seattle, along with lots of other information to help you enjoy the outdoors.

We would like to express our special thanks to Connie and Monty Moore of the Moore House Bed and Breakfast Inn. Connie prodded us to wade into this project, and and so the Moores befriended us, fed us, and housed us as we gathered information.

Thanks also to the entire Cle Elum Chamber of Commerce, without whom this book would not have been written, and especially to two Chamber presidents. Jennifer Grillo was president when this project was instigated, and took the idea to the Kittitas County Board of Commissioners and received their support. Peter Heide was president when the project was under way and shepherded it to completion. Both of them contributed a lot of time and energy to make this book a success.

Walking

Walking is one of the best ways to see where you are. You are going slowly enough to take in the sights, smells, and textures around you. And it is good exercise! Each of these walks has a different character. On Upper Peoh Point Road you are away from the town, and strolling through farmland. The Roslyn walk loops through town, visiting each corner, and the Cle Elum walk mixes a bit of town and a bit of country.

These walks were inspired by a special series of Volksmarches which used bed and breakfast inns all over the state as starting points. Volksports, are de-

fined as non-competitive, family-oriented, recreational, walking, swimming, bicycling, and cross-country ski events providing aerobic exercise that contributes to physical fitness,

Other popular places to walk are on pieces of the John Wayne Pioneer Trail in Iron Horse State Park. The Cle Elum Around Town Walk takes in a section of the trail which parallels town. You can simply continue farther in one direction once you are on the trail, or look in the Cross Country Ski section: John Wayne Pioneer Trail, for the piece east of town; and the Mountain Bike section: Iron Horse and Canal, for the trail description to the west.

Cle Elum Around Town Walk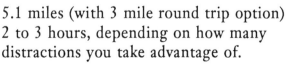
5.1 miles (with 3 mile round trip option)
2 to 3 hours, depending on how many
distractions you take advantage of.

Take a walk around Cle Elum, and enjoy the variety of a trip around a small town. Downtown there's the Telephone Museum, the bakery, and the oldest building in Cle Elum—the Key Bank building. Stop to take a look around. Then before you know it you've left the tidy houses and bright gardens behind, and you're in the woods. Then on to South Cle Elum—a completely separate town, with its own mayor and everything. It was the railroad center of the Upper Kittitas Valley, and in a way, it still is. The Moore House Bed and Breakfast Inn is practically a museum in honor of the men of the Milwaukee Road who took the trains over the Cascades, and who slept in the bunkhouse, which is now the Inn. Then pass the old depot, and on down to the rushing Yakima River, in a world apart from the populated places.

Take a picnic to the big city park, the river's edge, or to the little green spots with picnic tables downtown. That is another special thing about Cle Elum: there are two little parks in what used to be empty lots, tucked in between the old brick buildings on 1st St. Or stop in at one of the restaurants for a regular sit-down meal. Whichever way you take your sustenance, this walk offers lots of variety for a very pleasant couple of hours.

The Walk
Start on 1st St. and Pennsylvania Ave. Head east on 1st St. (away from the Cascade Mountains, and toward Ellensburg). Left on Peoh Ave. at the bakery. Left on 2nd St. Continue across the railroad tracks and up the hill (the one mile mark). Left on Reed St. just past the end of the guard rail. Follow Reed St. up to the city park. Left behind the backstop, and curve around to the right. There are restrooms available in the park. Left on Pine St.

Cross the highway. Left on Power St. towards the hospital. Continue past the new clinic. The large brick building on your right was the miner's hospital. Now look carefully—the route gets a little tricky here. Bear right at the end of the pavement of Power St., looking for the trail that angles left down the embankment. Take the trail down off the hill. Sharp right on Rossetti, and continue under the freeway, and over the Yakima River. (For a shorter trip of 3 miles total, turn left onto the dirt road along the Yakima River *before* crossing the river. Pick up the

instructions at mile 3.8.)

Right on Washington St. in South Cle Elum (mile 2). Curve around with the street. Continue on Main St., passing the South Cle Elum Firemen's Park. Left onto Milwaukee St. at the old railroad depot and electrical power plant. Milwaukee Road used the plant to power electric trains over the pass. There are plans for a museum in the depot.

Left on 6th St. The neighbor on the corner has a sign that makes 6th look like "West's Cozy Corner" (mile 3). Right on Broadway St. Left on 4th St., the main street through South Cle Elum. Continue past the Cle Elum Memorial Ball Park, and proceed to the river.

Cross the bridge, and at the end of the guard rail, turn right and follow the dirt road downstream along the river (mile 4). Take the left fork at the Y in the River Road (there's a pond on the left), leaving the river. Left on the paved road.

Cross the freeway and follow the paved road around to the left then right to Oaks Ave. Cross the RR tracks. Right on Railroad St. Left on Pennsylvania Ave. Right on 1st St., and you're done!

Roslyn and Its Cemeteries
3. 2 miles
1 1/2 hours, at least

Roslyn is a terrific place to walk. The town is full of history—from the original 1886 buildings downtown to the extraordinary Historical Cemeteries. The town was named a National Historic District in 1978, and the citizens have maintained an active interest in the history of their town. Roslyn came to life as a mining town, to provide the Milwaukee Road with coal for its steam locomotives, and attracted Central Europeans to work in the mines. The largest group were the Croatians, with Lithuanians, Slavonians, Yugoslavs, Italians, and others filling out the mixed citizenry. In 1888, the mining company brought 500 black miners from the east to break a strike, and Roslyn had a sizeable black population in its heyday. In the 1910s and '20s Roslyn had up to

7000 residents. Though the population was dropping anyway, after the last mine closed 1963, Roslyn's population settled at its current 900 residents. The population seems to be on the up-swing, however, with retired natives coming home, and younger people getting away from the urban pace on the west side of the mountains.

The town's fascinating cemeteries, grouped in a cluster on the edge of town, show the wide variety of ethnic groups and service organizations which maintained plots for their members. The cemeteries are now maintained by relatives, the Roslyn Kiwanis and history students at Cle Elum/Roslyn High School. The following list is made of bits and pieces of information gleaned from a series of detailed articles written by Karyne Ware as a Roslyn Kiwanis Club project.

The Roslyn Cemeteries: The cemeteries contain 26 separate but adjacent cemeteries covering 15 acres, with a total of about 5000 plots. The earliest graves date from 1887, and most of the cemeteries were founded before 1910. The ornate fences surrounding some of the plots were intended to protect the graves from cattle and wildlife.

Eagle's: Established in 1908, this cemetery is still maintained by the Eagles. One fellow interred here met his fate in 1928 when his 250 gallon moonshine still exploded. It was doubly unfortunate, as the ensuing fire burned thirty surrounding homes.

Polish: Only 24 headstones have been placed in this section, which was established in 1905. The most unusual feature of this cemetery is that all the plots are arranged north-south, not east-west as in all the other cemeteries.

St. Barbara's: The initials J.S.K.J. translated from Croatian stand for "Yugoslavian Catholic Lodge," and St. Barbara is the patron saint of those who work underground. Look for enamel portraits on the tombstones - an old country custom. The carving on George Liboky's marker was designed for him by his daughter, and the marker for a film maker with KING TV has a reel of film represented.

Redmen Lodge: The Redmen Lodge was organized as a charitable group and to "preserve American traditions"; the members wore Indian motif uniforms to meetings. Little is known about the order, but it is unlikely that it was a Native Americans' organization.

Knights of Pythias: Many of the markers are adorned with symbols of the order: doves, crossed swords, and letters representing secret rituals. One set of letters is known: "FCB" stands for "Friendship, Charity, Bravery," the motto of the order. There is nearly an entire row for those killed in a mine disaster on May 10, 1892.

Sokol Lodge: This is the smallest cemetery with only two graves are visible, though some old-timers remember more. The Lodge was organized in 1914 among the Yugoslavs to promote patriotism and athletic skill. Men's and women's gymnastic teams performed throughout the area.

Dr. Starcevic #1: The Croatian community established this cemetery in 1904 and named it for a patriot who had recently struggled successfully against an imposed ruler in their homeland. The markers resemble those in the old country more than any other in the Roslyn Cemeteries. Dr. Starcevic #2 was named so when two Croatian fraternal orders merged in 1927.

Other cemeteries include the Veteran's, City, Lithuanian, Old County, Mason's, Oddfellows, Moose, Cacciatori d'Africa, Druid's, Forester's, Silvio Pellico, Mt. Olivet, and Serbian.

Drive from Cle Elum:
Head westbound on 2nd Ave. in Cle Elum. Continue about two and a half miles on Hwy. 903 to the center of Roslyn. Park near the central intersection of 1st and Pennsylvania.

The Walk:
Head north on Pennsylvania Ave. (turn right as you arrive from Cle Elum). The oldest continuously operating tavern in the state is the Brick Tavern on the corner. The company store of the

Northwestern Improvement Company, built in 1916, is kitty-corner from the tavern. Left on N.B. (North "B") St. at the 3-way fork where the Plum Creek buildings are straight ahead. Pass Immaculate Conception Catholic Church first built in 1887, and rebuilt in 1932 after a fire. Left on Utah Ave. Cross 1st St. (use caution, it is Hwy. 903). Watch for the first building in Roslyn, a log cabin built in 1885. Right on 2nd St. Cross Nevada Ave. (Hwy. 903). Left on the next street, which is Alaska Ave., but is unmarked.

Left at the stop sign onto the highway, which is 7th St. Straight on 7th Ave where the highway turns. Curve around to the left onto Utah Ave. Right on 3rd St. Straight past the school, Pioneer Park, and Slim Runje Field. Curve around to the left onto Washington Ave. Right on 2nd St. Right on Pennsylvania Ave.

The museum, on your right, is well worth 50 cents for a visit. It is open 7 days a week in the summer, and if it happens to be closed when you pass by, one of the local shopkeepers will call Mary Osmonovich Andler, the curator, and most likely she'll open it for you.

Continue on Pennsylvania Ave. Right on 4th St. Left on 7th St. Continue straight back into the woods as the road turns to dirt. You will enter the Roslyn Cemeteries through the back door. Explore the cemeteries on the upper tier, and continue down the hill to the paved road. Left on the paved road running through the cemeteries. Straight on the dirt road; stop for a look at the map of the cemeteries and the old photos, then continue alongside the Veterans' Cemetery with its white markers. Continue past the new cemetery.

Curve to the left as the road becomes paved. Right at the yield sign onto unmarked 3rd St. On the way up the hill, take a break and look back down across Roslyn. You can also see mine tailings to the north. Curve to the left onto California Ave. Left on 2nd St. Continue into the center of Roslyn. Right on Pennsylvania Ave. Arrive where you started.

Peoh Point Roads Walk

8 miles (with a 3 mile round trip option)
3 hours

Peoh Point rises above Cle Elum to the south. Peoh Point Roads (Upper and Lower) cross the agricultural land below the Point. Look over, to the rocky promontory lifting up from the valley floor. If you look very closely at the rugged crest, you can see Peoh Point Lookout: a fire lookout and weather station operated by the State Department of Natural Resources. Besides having a constant view of Peoh Point as you walk this route, the Stuart Mountains poke their ragged peaks up to the north. And up close, the green pastures are just as attractive in their calming way. The route parallels the irrigation canal for a time; it is an engineered gully running from Lake Easton to Ellensburg, deep and full of clear mountain water running down an ever-so-slight grade to bring the desert to life. Finish the loop on the John Wayne PioneerTrail in Iron Horse State Park, the longest (25 miles) and skinniest (some 30 feet) state park around.

Drive:

Start at First St and Pennsylvania Ave. Go west on First St. Cross the railroad tracks. Left at the Y towards South Cle Elum. Continue across the Yakima River. This road becomes 4th St in South Cle Elum. Continue on 4th through town, and follow it as it turns left and becomes lower Peoh Point Road. Park in the large gravel lot on the left at the bottom of the hill.

The Eight Mile Walk:

Head up the hill on Lower Peoh Point Rd. Right on Upper Peoh Point Rd. at the top of the hill. Bear left at the Y, staying on Upper Peoh Point Rd. at the junction with Mohar Rd. Left on the canal frontage trail *just before* crossing the

7

concrete bridge over the canal.

Stay on the canal trail as it crosses Upper Peoh Point Rd. Left on Markovich Rd. at the next intersection. Right on Upper Peoh Point Rd. Left on Watson Cutoff Rd. Left on Lower Peoh Point Rd, at the end of Watson Cutoff Rd. After a few yards, the John Wayne Trail is visible on your right. It is an 10-foot-wide gravel path which used to be a railroad track. Cut over to the trail, and continue in the same direction. Continue on the trail until you reach the parking lot, on your left.

For a shorter walk in the same area, try this loop. It doesn't use either the canal road or the John Wayne Pioneer Trail, but it travels the lightly used roads on the bench above town. Park in the same place as the longer walk above.

The Three Mile Walk:
Head uphill on Lower Peoh Point Rd. Right on Upper Peoh Point Rd. Left on Pays Rd. at the fire station. Left on Lower Peoh Point Rd. (not to be confused with nearby Groeschell Rd.) Arrive back at the parking lot.

Hiking

One special thing about hiking in Upper Kittitas County is the easy access to the Alpine Lakes Wilderness. You bump into it at the end of every northbound road, it seems. Two of the hikes here are in the Wilderness. Remember that when you go into the Wilderness, you must leave dogs and mechanical means of transport (that includes bicycles) at the front door, and enter with a commitment to tread lightly.

Carry plenty of water (unless you have the means to purify it), food, and warm clothing. The two trails into the Wilderness gain significant altitude, and the air is noticeably cooler at times.

For more ideas on hiking trails in the area, stop by the Cle Elum Ranger District Office, west of central Cle Elum on Second St. (also Hwy.903). Pick up your copy of the Mountain View Gazette while you're there. They also have an updated trail guide and a small bookstore of topics ranging from rocks to routes to flowers. One of the most comprehensive trail guidebooks is the Mountaineers *102 Hikes in the Alpine Lakes, South Cascades, and Olympics*, text by Ira Spring and Harvey Manning, photos by Bob and Ira Spring.

Cooper River Trail

7 miles round trip
4 hours
High Point: 2950'
Elevation Gain: 450'
June through October

The beautiful Cooper River is the main attraction of this hike. The

river, flowing through a lovely forest with the trail hugging the hillside along its banks, has a splendid blue-green color and gorgeous pools. Cooper Lake, at the turn-around, is also very beautiful. If seven miles isn't enough, take an excursion along the lake's edge on a trail which continues the length of the lake.

The trail is rarely very steep, and though the round trip is seven miles, it is a relatively easy seven. The elevation gain to the lake is 450'. The trail is popular, and you will likely meet other hikers, and maybe some mountain bicyclists.

A road goes to the lake, so with a little logistics planning, a group could hike one way and have someone pick them up. Or some in the group could hike both ways, and others only one. And plan on a picnic at Owhi Campground on the shores of Cooper Lake!

Drive:
Take Hwy. 903 along Cle Elum Lake, to Salmon la Sac. Cross the bridge towards the campground, and turn right on the dirt road. Continue for about 1/2 mile to the trailhead. There is no water at the trailhead, so pick some up at Salmon la Sac on the way in.

To drive to Cooper Lake, go back out of Salmon la Sac the way you came in. In one mile turn right [west] on Forest Service Road #46. In 5 miles turn right on Road #4616, crossing over the Cooper River. The trail appears on your right just across the bridge; Owhi Campground is another quarter mile beyond.

The Hike:
Three trails start together at the trailhead and split after about 100 yards; just follow the Cooper River Trail (#1311) sign, keeping to the left. Follow the trail to the lake (continuing along the lake if you like) and return.

Kachess Ridge and Silver Creek Trail
12 miles round trip
8 hours
High Point: 5100'
Elevation Gain: 2700'
Early May through October

The variety of scenery along this trail is second to none. It starts along Silver Creek in a very narrow river canyon and quickly moves up into an open hillside, with glimpses into the lower Silver Creek Gorge and south into the Yakima River valley. The scenery above

the gorge, where the creek flattens out, turns into large old growth timber, inter-spersed with small meadows. Further along and near the upper limits of this stream, you'll be dazzled by the lush, high mountain meadows, wildflowers, silvery snags and rocky peaks. There is an excellent opportunity for the quiet hiker to observe deer, elk and mountain goats in this basin.

Drive:

From I-90, exit 70, go north for .3 mile to road 4818, then east on road 4818-203 for .7 mile (under the powerline), then left at the small wood sign (sometimes the sign is missing) and dirt road heading north across the powerline and into the forest, and travel .3 mile to the trailhead.

The Hike:

The trail starts at the small unimproved trailhead, and climbs steadily for one mile to the basin at the top of the gorge. From there the grade lessens, but still climbs steadily, paralleling Silver Creek, until it passes through a saddle and out of this basin.

If you want to ascend only to the closest view point, when you first enter the timber above the gorge look for Kachess Beacon Trail, to the left. It climbs to an abandoned FAA Beacon site, with excellent views of the Yakima River Valley and the surrounding hills. Return the way you came.

This area is not in a Congressionally designated Wilderness, but it still provides an opportunity for solitude and the feeling of a primitive experience. This trail is open to hiking, pack and saddle stock, and mountain bikes. It is closed to motorized vehicles.

 *Hiking*

Paddy-Go-Easy Pass
7 1/2 miles round trip
About 4 hours
High Point 6100'
Elevation Gain 2700'
Mid-July through September

The view from Paddy-Go-Easy Pass spreads out in all directions. Majestic peaks deeper in the mountains, and the Cle Elum Valley out towards the plains. Because the elevation is high, the flowers are blooming in July—springtime in the alpine meadows. An easy quarter-mile from the top of the pass, Sprite Lake tempts you down for a side trip to the lake's edge. The hike up to the pass is steep, but because the distance is not great, you can take it easy and still have plenty of time at the top.

Drive:
Take Hwy. 903 through Roslyn to Salmon la Sac. Continue on Forest Service Rd. #4330 11 miles, about a half mile past the Fish Lake guard station. Find the trail-head, #1595, on your right, amongst a cluster of cabins.

The Hike:
Head up and enter the Alpine Lakes Wilderness Area in about a mile. A little past that point, keep left when you reach a fork in the trail; the right fork goes back down to the guard station. At the next fork, at about 2 1/2 miles, you can go either way; the routes join about a quarter of a mile below the pass. From Paddy-Go-Easy Pass, continue southward (basically to your right) to Sprite Lake, and take a jaunt down to the shore. Return the way you came.

Road Bicycling

Bicycling in Upper Kittitas is really great for a couple of reasons. One is that it is beautiful, with lakes, green fields, and stunning views to the mountains. Another good thing is that the roads are very quiet; usually residents are the only traffic passing by. And of course, most of the paved roads run the length the valley, and so there aren't any big hills. Just a few little ones to keep things interesting and let you shift gears sometimes.

Besides the four routes described in this section, the driving loop to Thorp is a beautiful ride. It is a popular trip with cyclists in Ellensburg, as well as groups from the west side of the mountains. For some shorter rides, try the walking routes. You'll encounter short sections of dirt road on each of the walks.

Roslyn and Cle Elum Lake
22 Miles Round Trip
695' Elevation Gain
2 hours

Roslyn is a wonderful destination in itself. In fact, if that is only as far as you get, that's okay. The Roslyn Historic Cemeteries are worth the trip. There are 26 different cemeteries in 15 acres, most were created by ethnic benevolent fraternal organizations. See the Roslyn Walk for more information. Wish Poosh Campground is a great place for a picnic, and if you feel energetic, you can continue along the lake shore. Salmon la Sac is another 9 miles or so (making a total of 40 miles). As the road to Salmon la Sac is rebuilt piece by piece in the the coming few years, a good shoulder will appear, piece by piece.

0.0	Start at First St. and Pennsylvania Ave. in Cle Elum. Head north on Pennsylvania.
0.1	Left on Second Ave. You are now heading towards the mountains.
0.3	Cross RR track, head uphill.
1.8	Right onto the paved road across from the high school (not marked).
2.7	Right on S. A St.
3.0	Bear left with the street - pass an auto scrap yard.
3.1	Right on the main road through town - S. First St.
3.4	Left on Pennsylvania St. in Roslyn. Continue straight past 4th Ave.
3.6	Follow to the right onto 5th Ave.
3.7	Left on Memorial Rd.
3.9	Visit Roslyn Historical Cemeteries.
5.3	Left onto Hwy. 903 - the main road through Ronald.
5.9	Bear left out of town.
7.6	Left on S. Lake Cabins Rd.
8.2	Right on the next street (unmarked).
8.3	Left on another unmarked street just as highway comes into sight.
8.5	Left on the highway.
9.7	Pass the Skookum Inn, Last Resort Restaurant, and small grocery store.
10.5	Left into Wish Poosh Campground. Head out to the picnic island in the park. Return to the highway.
11.3	Right on the highway.
13.4	Right on N. Lake Cabins Rd.
13.7	Right on S. Lake Cabins Rd.
14.3	Left to the highway.
14.4	Right on the highway.
16	Right on Arctic Ave.
16.1	Left on 3rd Ave.
16.4	Right on Fanhouse Rd. Pass the Cemeteries again.
18.0	Bear left onto Memorial Rd.
18.2	Right on 5th Ave.

14

Bear left onto Pennsylvania Ave.
18.4 Right on 2nd Ave.
Pass streets named for the
western states.
19 Bear left on Hoffmanville St.
Straight across the highway.
19.1 Right on S. A St.
19.2 Left on South St.
20.1 Left on Hwy. 97.
22.1 Right on Pennsylvania Ave.
22.2 Arrive at First St. and Pennsylvania Ave. in Cle Elum.

Easton Lake State Park and Return

35 Miles Round Trip
635' Elevation Gain
3-4 hours

Easton Lake State Park is a lovely, shady, big park. The green-blue lake shimmers behind a curtain of native coniferous trees. Paths wind through the forest along the lake shore, beckoning the cyclist to slow even further, and enjoy a stroll.

The back roads between Cle Elum and Easton travel through lovely rolling terrain, with very little traffic. Pack your collapsible fishing pole, your swimsuit, or just a snack for a little diversion at the lake. There are some trails around the lake shore, so you can do a little exploring. The route uses the shoulder of I-90 just the distance between two exits. We think the rest of the route is worth the noise of riding the shoulder a short way.

An interesting feature along the route is the major irrigation canal which is fed by Lake Easton. The canal maintains an even and very slight grade down to the lower Kittitas Valley. You cross the canal four times on your way to Lake Easton—the first time is on Reservoir

Canyon Rd. The canal is in a huge concrete pipe, and it dips down from one side of the canyon, passes under the road, and climbs back up the other. The strength of the flow and gravity send the water down more than a hundred feet, and back up the other side. The canal then resumes its open river-like appearance. You'll see it three times more, out in the open. It is very pretty, but don't swim in it, as it is moving fast, and offers few opportunities to get out along its smooth banks.

0.0 Start at First St and Pennsylvania Ave. Cross the railroad tracks.
0.4 Left at the Y towards South Cle Elum
     Continue across the Yakima River. This road becomes 4th St. in South Cle Elum.
1.2 Right on Madison St.
1.3 Left on 6th St. at the four way stop.
     Continue out of town turning right, then left, as the road becomes Reservoir Canyon Road.
3.5 Pass Mohar Rd., and Reservoir Canyon Rd. becomes Westside Rd.
8.5 Cross the canal, and go straight as Bernardo Rd. goes to the right
8.7 Straight to continue on Nelson Siding Rd.
12.3 Cross the Iron Horse Trail, and go under I-90.
     There is a fishing access and restroom at Lavendar Lake on the other side of the interchange.
12.6 Left onto I-90 Westbound.
     At the blue "Food Ahead" sign you can walk across the buffer zone, lift your bike over a low cable, and ride on the frontage road.
14.9 Exit 71 to Easton.
15.0 Cross the freeway on the overpass.
15.2 Right on the main street in Easton at the stop sign.
15.9 Left into Lake Easton State Park.
16.0 Right towards the picnic area.
17.0 Arrive at the picnic area and small swimming beach
18.0 Exit the park by turning right.
     Continue through town.
18.8 Left towards I-90.
18.9 Right onto I-90.
21.2 Right off of I-90 at the next exit, #74, West Nelson Siding Road.
21.4 Right at the end of the ramp onto West Nelson Siding Road (not marked here).
     Cross the railroad tracks and the Iron Horse State Park.
25.2 Stay on the low road at the Y. You came down the hill, but there's

a better way up!

25.7 Right at the T onto Bernardo Rd. (not marked).

26.2 Left on Westside Rd. at the top of the hill.
Cross the canal.

27.1 Keep left in the tight curve to stay on Westside Rd. - the other is not paved.
Continue on Westside Rd., and go down the big hill. The biggest siphon in the area is at mile 31.5.

33.3 Left on 6th St. in South Cle Elum.

33.5 Right on Madison St.

33.7 Left on 4th St.
Cross the Yakima River, and under I-90.

34.4 Curve to the right at the Y, and continue into downtown Cle Elum.

34.8 Arrive at Pennsylvania Ave. and First St. in Cle Elum.

Teanaway Valley and West Fork Swimming Hole

34 Miles
360' Elevation Gain
3-4 hours

The Teanaway Valley is truly one of the serene and beautiful places in the state of Washington. Open fields are hemmed in by tree-covered hills, and the farms seem to look the same as in years gone by. Each season has its own special beauty here. Then, up past the farms, you duck into the woods, and follow the west fork of the Teanaway River to a quiet spot off the paved road. The river flows over a smooth rock bed, forming round pools in places, and in others covering the polished rock by only inches.

0 Head east on First St. at Pennsylvania Ave.

1   Left at the Y where 90 Business Loop turns right out of town. Follow the road around to the right

1.5   Left on Cle Elum Airport Rd.
      Straight on Airport Rd. until it bears right

4.1   Next left on W. Masterson Rd.
      Take W. Masterson Rd. as it bears right to the yield sign and

5.2   Turn left on E. Masterson Rd.

7.4   Start 3/4 mile of gravel road.

8.6   Left on Teanaway Rd.

14.7 Teanaway Mercantile; snacks.

15.3 Left turn onto West Fork Teanaway Rd. You can see the Stuart Range to your right.
      Go straight to continue on West Fork Teanaway Rd. (Middle Fork goes to the right.)

16.5 Pavement ends.
      Left at the Y

16.6 Straight as a heavily-used logging road curves left. The road is smooth, compact dirt with little traffic.

17   As you parallel the West Fork Teanaway River, look over to choose a swimming hole or a nice place for a rest and something to eat.
      Go back out the W. Fork Teanaway Rd.

18.7 Right on Teanaway Rd.

25.4 Right on E. Masterson Rd.

28.8 Right on W. Masterson Rd.

29.9 Right on Cle Elum Airport Rd. at the T.

32.5 Right at the next T, and continue as the road bears to the left.

33   Continue straight onto First St.

34   Arrive back at First St. and Pennsylvania Ave.

Upper and Lower Peoh Point Roads Loop
13 Miles Round Trip
425' Elevation Gain
1 1/2 hours

Peoh Point Road is named after the prominent rock outcropping to the south which rises above the valley floor. The State main-

tains a fire lookout and weather station on the point, and it is staffed in the summer months. This route does not go up there, thank goodness! Rather, it rolls along on the flank of the valley, through farms and hay fields. The roads carry very little traffic, and the Stuart Mountains rise above the far side of the valley.

0.0 Start at First St. and Pennsylvania Ave. Go west on First St. Cross the railroad tracks.
0.4 Left at the Y towards South Cle Elum.
Continue across the Yakima River. This road becomes 4th St. in South Cle Elum.
Continue straight on 4th through town until the road turns left and becomes Lower Peoh Point Rd.
4.1 Right on Watson Cutoff Rd.
5.2 Right on Upper Peoh Point Rd. You can see Peoh Point Lookout up ahead on the left on the high rock outcropping.
7.0 You can see Roslyn across the valley, ahead and to the right.
7.8 Left on Mohar Rd.
9.7 Right on Reservoir Canyon Rd.
11.7 Bear to the left onto 6th St. as you enter South Cle Elum.
Right at the first stop sign, onto Madison St.
12.1 Left on 4th St.
Cross the Yakima River.
12.9 Right at the Y, and continue onto First St.
13.3 Arrive at First St. and Pennsylvania Ave.

Mountain Biking

Mountain bikes are what brought us to Cle Elum in the first place. We marveled at the miles and miles of wonderful roads and trails. Meadows, rocky outcroppings, and lookout towers with astounding views are scattered liberally throughout Upper Kittitas County. Here are three rides to whet your appetite. Look in our *Guide to Mountain Bike Riding in Washington*, available in book stores and bike shops all over the state, for more places to try.

Cooper River Trail, in the hiking section of this book, is a very nice mountain bike ride. We suggest you ride on the road up to Cooper Lake, and ride the trail down, though it is rideable in both directions. Read the Red Top drive for special instructions for doing the route on a mountain bike, with a shorter total distance. For the very ambitious, the Quartz Mountain motorcycle trip could be an overnight ride, stopping at the campground at Quartz Mountain. Check out the Taneum Trails motorcycle ride as well.

Peoh Point Lookout

Miles: 20 (26 via alternate return route)
Elevation Gain: 1200' (1800' for alternate)
High Point: 4020'
Travel Time: 3 hours (4 for alternate)

Peoh Point Lookout is one of our favorite discoveries by mountain bike. It sits on a rocky promontory south of I-90, and is clearly visible as you drive on the Interstate. From the lookout, the view is northward over Cle Elum and the upper Yakima River valley. The view extends well beyond the valley to the Stuart Range and spectacular peaks in the Alpine Lakes Wilderness. Peoh Point is a great driving destination, too, but the alternate route down is for two-wheeled vehicles only!

Two sign corrections must be made: 1) The sign at the bottom that says "Peoh Pt. 10 m." is wrong—it is only 8 miles. 2) The sign at the lookout that says "Elev. 3715" is wrong—it is actually 4020 feet. So you don't have to go as far as they say, and you will have worked harder than they give you credit for!

The alternate route down takes a loop to the east, traveling at an even elevation for the first 7 miles after leaving the lookout. Then you go up about 600 feet, and finally lose all the elevation you gained on the way up to Peoh Point. We think that the extra distance is well worth the time—the views to the south and the easy terrain combine to make the alternate a very pleasant one. The alternate ends with about 5 miles on pavement.

Drive:
Start at First St. and Pennsylvania Ave. Go west on First St. Cross the railroad tracks. Left at the Y towards South Cle Elum. Continue across the Yakima River. This road becomes 4th St. in

South Cle Elum. Right on Madison St. Left on 6th St. at the four way stop. Right on Milwaukee St. Park in the Iron Horse State Park trailhead on your left. (1.5 miles from the center of Cle Elum.)

The Ride:
Go back out to 6th St. and turn right. Continue 2 miles on what has become Canyon Reservoir Rd. Take the third left onto Forest Service Rd. 3350. You will see the sign to Peoh Point.

Continue up for 6 miles. At the big intersection at the top (Five Corners) turn left onto Rd. 115. At 7 miles keep left on the better traveled road. At 7.5 miles go around the gate and continue another .5 mile out to the lookout. Return the same way, or take the following alternate route down.

Alternate Return:
Start back from the lookout and pass the gate. At the three-way fork in 1 mile turn left onto the middle road, Rd. 114. Do not take Rd. 116. Straight across onto Rd. 3350 at the four-way intersection in another mile. At 10.5 miles pass Taneum Point. Pass Osborn Point at 13 miles. When you come around the corner from Osborn Point to face north, you can see a  microwave tower on the next ridge. You will be passing by the foot of the tower. Right at the T where Rd. 3352 goes left at mile 14.

At mile 15 turn left on the first major road leading uphill. You have passed some other logging cuts, but nothing so obviously permanent as this. It is marked with a green dot, there is a green dot on the road you've been on, and there is a small arrow sign facing the other way on the right on the far side of the intersection. Since the road is not marked any other way, watch for these clues.

Pass an inoperative gate. At mile 15.5 arrive at the top of the hill at the base of the telephone microwave tower you could see from the other ridge. Keep left at the fork of two equally travelled roads a mile and a half down from the top. Continue down to the right as you enter the upper reaches of Sky Meadows, a summer house community. Left on Taneum Creek Rd. at a four-way intersection.

Keep right around the community center and swimming pool area. Take a moment to look at the view.

At 20.5 turn left on Upper Peoh Point Rd. at the stop sign, and cross the canal. (You can get on the canal road by turning left on the far side of the canal.. Continue, crossing the road one more time, then get off at the second crossing. Keep going west on Upper Peoh Point Rd.) Left at the T on Lower Peoh Point Rd. Left on Madison Ave. in South Cle Elum. Left on 6th St., and right on Milwaukee to the parking lot.

Cle Elum Ridge Loop

37 miles - 17 paved miles; 20 off-road miles
Elevation Gain 1850'
6 hours

This is a fun ride with lots of variety, though it is for cyclists who are in pretty good shape. Thirty-seven miles is a long way, and 20 dirt miles requires a good effort in itself. However, a person new to mountain biking can enjoy this loop because the terrain doesn't demand a lot of fancy bike handling skills. The route is interesting because you're not on full-fledged logging roads the whole way, either; they're something like jeep trails.

Once you get up to Cle Elum Ridge, you can see down both sides. Roslyn, Ronald and Cle Elum sit nestled alongside the Yakima River on one side, and the forest spreads out on the other. Take little branch trails out to viewpoints here and there along the way. Most of the dirt road section is on land which belongs to Plum Creek. Take care to leave gates as you found them, and remember that you're a guest in this area. We want mountain bikers to be welcome here far into the future.

The Ride:
From the center of Cle Elum head east on First St. Left at the Y where 90 Business Loop turns right out of town. Follow the road around to the right. Left on Cle Elum Airport Rd. Continue on Airport Rd. as it bears right. Left on West Masterson Rd. Continue

on West Masterson as it bears right to the yield sign and then turn left on East Masterson Rd. Continue across 3/4 mile of gravel.

Left on Teanaway Road at the T, at mile 8.5. At mile 14.7 pass Teanaway Mercantile: pop, beer, water, snack food, bait. At last word open 7 days a week, about 10 am to 8 pm. Left onto West Teanaway Road. You can see the Stuart Range to the right. Go straight to continue on the West Fork Teanaway River Road (Middle Fork Road goes to the right). At mile 16.5 the pavement ends.

Keep right at the Y. If you take a side trip on the left fork, you parallel the river, and in much less than a mile you come to a great swimming hole; an ideal place to enjoy a dip or a snack. If you look off to the left you can see a knoll that has been logged off. It is on the Cle Elum Ridge road you will be on; look down to the meadow you're in now when you get up there. The road is washed out at mile 19.5. You can scurry along the bank and save one ford, but your feet are probably going to get wet anyway. Ford the river again.

Left onto the Dingbat Creek Road at mile 20.2. The clues are a bridge that is out (you will have to ford the river again), a signpost with no signs, and the beginnings of a log house. Stay to the left fork after you pass the log house. Pass a hunting hut called the Teanaway Hilton. Pass through an open gate. There are lots of ORV trail crossings; stay on the main road. At mile 22.5, go through a closed gate, and close it behind you. Turn left into what looks like a gully, it's the main road. Bear left with the road, and crest the hill. This area was logged in 1989.

Okay, watch carefully now! As the road starts to go down steeply, turn left and go up steeply onto a more minor road. Don't go downhill. You are now on Cle Elum Ridge. There are nice views of Cle Elum Lake from up here. Cross over a big berm at the edge of the clearcut, and get on the old road. Bear right and continue along the crest of the ridge. At a big intersection there is an old mine and and ruins of something. A major road comes up from the valley.

Continue along the crest. At a major Y in the road at mile 31.3, keep left, down a gully and up a rutted hill. (Our map shows that the right fork comes out in Cle Elum, too.) Pass two fenced-in antennas on the left.

Keep to the right as you start to go down off the ridge. Stay on the best traveled road and keep going down. Continue through the back neighborhoods of Cle Elum until you get to First St. Right on First St. to your starting point.

Iron Horse State Park and Canal Road
Miles: 31 (with 16 mile round-trip option)
Elevation Gain: 300'
4 hours

The Iron Horse State Park is home to about 30 miles of the John Wayne Pioneer Trail from west of Easton nearly to Thorp. The John Wayne Trail stretches a total of 213 miles across Eastern Washington on the

old Milwaukee Railroad right of way. Call the state Department of Natural Resources at (509) 925-6131 for more information about using the John Wayne Trail outside of the Iron Horse State Park.

In the Iron Horse State Park, cyclists, walkers, equestrians and skiers enjoy the unspoiled scenery along the Yakima River. The grade is almost imperceptible from Cle Elum to Easton as the route travels up a mere 200'. The route back travels along an irrigation canal which parallels the trail. The canal crosses under roads by entering a big tube, called a siphon, which dives down below the road grade, then rises back on the other side. The water pressure created by the drop is spent getting

the water back up the other side. There are no pumps or other devices - just the tube. In the spring the canal is full and fast. In the fall it is entirely different, carrying a slow trickle, if that.

Drive:

Start at First St. and Pennsylvania Ave. Go west on First St. Cross the railroad tracks. Left at the Y towards South Cle Elum, just before the

road rises out of town. Continue across the Yakima River. This road becomes 4th St. in South Cle Elum. Right on Madison St. Left on 6th St. at the four way stop. Right on Milwaukee St. Park at the Iron Horse State Park trailhead on your left. (1.5 miles from the center of Cle Elum.)

The Ride:

Right onto the trail, and continue on the trail for over 15 miles, crossing two bridges and passing through rather isolated countryside.

For a shorter ride, with a total of about 16 miles: Turn left off of the trail onto Bernardo Road. It is the first paved road after the golf course. (You'll see an I-90 interchange to your right.) Left on Westside Road at the yield sign. IMMEDIATE left onto the canal road, before crossing the bridge. Pick up the instructions below, one mile before Peterson Siphon)

Continue past the trailhead parking lot at the Easton end. Easy left when you get to the pavement at mile 15.5. Take the unmarked roadway between Cabin Creek Rd. on the right and 2nd Ave. on the left. At mile 17.7 turn left at the T onto the dirt road along the canal - to the right you can see an old paved road.

Pass cross roads and siphon underpasses. Arrive at Peterson Siphon at mile 23.5. Follow to the right to continue. The road leaves the canal for a total of half a mile to get around. Left on the pavement onto Westside Rd. Keep left on the pavement to continue back towards the canal. Cross the canal and turn right on the canal road.

At mile 26 you arrive at a big siphon. Bear left and continue downhill in the same direction you have been following along the canal . Mile 27.5: cross Westside Rd. In one mile bear right across the front of the biggest siphon so far, and double back along the other side of the canal. Continue to the left out to the paved road.

Left on Westside Rd., and go down! Watch for the siphon as it passes under the road, which by now is called Reservoir Canyon Rd. Cross the John Wayne Trail Pioneer in South Cle Elum. Left on Milwaukee Ave. to the trailhead.

Driving

One wonderful thing about Upper Kittitas County is that you can hike, bicycle, or ski to beautiful and special places. The really great thing about the area is that you can also drive to most of those places. All of the routes suggested here are suitable for a passenger car, and all of the roads are well maintained by the Wenatchee National Forest or Kittitas County. Some routes use paved roads and others gravel roads; some are short and will take only part of the morning, and others are all-day excursions.

When you drive into the forest, you get a long way from help in a hurry. Be sure your car is in good condition, that you have plenty of gas, and use extra caution while traveling on one-lane roads in the mountains. In the spring and fall, check snow conditions before heading out on Red Top or Lion Rock; both get up pretty high.

Besides these routes which are specifically described as drives, there are a few nice drives in other sections of this book. Quartz Mountain, in the Motorcycling section, is terrific. Go up and back the same way (the motorcyclists return on trails). Stop by Peoh Point Lookout while you're so close (see the description in the Mountain Biking section).

A trip to Salmon la Sac, along Cle Elum Lake is a basic ingredient in a complete visit to Upper Kittitas County. Just take Hwy. 903 west out of Cle Elum, passing through Roslyn (don't miss the cemeteries) and Ronald on the way. Take a walk around

Salmon la Sac Campground, or start up the Cooper River Trail (see the Hiking section). There are some very pretty pools near the beginning of the trail.

Thorp and Yakima River Canyon
40.5 Miles (all paved)
One hour driving time
High Point: 2000'

The loop to Thorp takes in a wide variety of terrain and activity in the Kittitas Valley. Cle Elum is surrounded by trees, and the folks there make their living from them. Just a bit farther down the valley, however, the trees thin out, and finally disappear. Then ranching and hay growing takes over. Stuart Anderson's ranch is along this route. Thorp is a quiet town with a couple of businesses, but it looks like most of the neighbors go into Ellensburg for their essentials. An old grain mill (or so it seems) is being restored, the grocery store and tavern look well established, and the houses and gardens make it look like the residents like it here. Interstate 90 hems the town in on the south side, and near the freeway entrance is a huge fruit-vegetable-antique market.

This beautiful and productive valley owes its livelihood to the Yakima River, which provides the water to make it all grow. The return trip takes you close to the river, up an interesting canyon full of volcanic basalt, thanks to Mt. Rainier many millennia ago. On a hot day, the river may seem attractive to a parched traveler, but I would recommend a place other than the canyon for a dip, as the river is moving quite fast through here. Finally, enter Cle Elum through the back door, past hay fields and the local airport.

To extend the drive by about 25 miles, turn right onto Hwy. 970 at the end of Hwy. 10 (after Thorp and the canyon road), then left in about 4 miles onto Teanaway River Rd. Then follow the instructions written out in the Bicycle Road Riding section. The Teanaway River Valley is one of the loveliest places in Upper Kittitas County.

The Drive:
Head west on First St. out of Cle Elum. Cross the railroad tracks. Left at the Y towards South Cle Elum. Continue across the Yakima

River. This road becomes 4th St. in South Cle Elum. Continue straight on 4th through town until the road turns left and becomes Lower Peoh Point Rd. Right on Watson Cutoff Rd. Left on Upper Peoh Point Rd. at the T.

At mile 8, cross I-90 and follow to the right. What a view of the  Stuart Range! The road becomes Thorp Prairie Rd. There is a modern windmill on the left, but we have never seen it working. Bear left onto the Taneum Road at mile 15.5. Right on the Thorp Highway at the T. Enter Thorp. There is a park one mile out of town: continue almost to the I-90 interchange, and turn left, following the sign to Gladmar Park. You could round out your lunch at the fruit and antique market near I-90. You will also cross the Iron Horse State Park here.

Turn around and go back through Thorp. Pass the Taneum Road and continue along the river on the Thorp Highway. Cross the Yakima River and continue straight. Left on Highway 10. The river canyon here has impressive rock formations. You can see the John Wayne Trail on the opposite side of the river; it looks like a dirt road. Pass through Bristol, recognizable only by the railroad sign.

Left on highway 97. Immediate right on West Masterson Rd. Continue straight at the stop sign. The road becomes Cle Elum Airport Rd. Right at the T. Continue straight at the stop sign into Cle Elum.

Red Top Lookout and the Teanaway River Valley

60 Miles (24 gravel)
High Point: 5361'
2 1/2 hours driving time

Red Top is famous among rockhounds for its agates. Bring your spade if you want to try your luck. The parking lot just below the lookout can accommodate a million cars (or so), there is a picnic table, and the outhouse is posted, "Comfort Station Donated by the Washington State Mineral Council, 1973." These are not the only signs of activity—the favorite hounding area is called the "Battleground" because of the huge craters left by decades of excavation.

The lookout tower and the house still exist although they haven't been used for years. The tower is a steep 1/2 mile up a trail from the parking lot. The view of Mt. Stuart and the Stuart Range from Red Top is one of the best we know. Mt. Rainier stands in the distance, and Mt. Adams peeks over the closer hills. Peoh Point Lookout is clearly visible if you know where to look (see the Peoh Point Lookout ride in the Mountain Biking section, then go up there in your car). You can also see Table Mountain to the east—a long columnar basalt cliff. Lion Rock is there, and the drive description is in this book.

This is a great destination for mountain biking, and with a bike you can take a route down which uses a piece of trail, and makes a shorter loop. Park either at the junction of Hwy. 97 and Rd. 9738 (total distance 14 miles), or save 4 miles and park up the hill at the junction of Rd. 9738 and Rd.9702. In either case, follow the driving instructions up to the lookout. Continue on your bike on the trail towards the lookout to the Y where the sign says Red Top straight; agate beds to the right. Leave your bike here, take the 1 mile round trip to the lookout, and then continue to the agate beds on your bike. Ride through the Battleground, and out the other side. Continue into the woods and down to the T. Turn left (downhill). Make a hard right onto Rd. 9738. Continue 3.5 miles to Rd. 9702, and another 2 miles down to Hwy. 97.

The Drive:

Head east on 1st St. in Cle Elum. Keep left at the I-90 interchange, continuing on Hwy. 970 towards Wenatchee. Keep left at the

intersection with Hwy. 10, continuing on Hwy. 970 towards Wenatchee. Straight at the junction with Hwy. 97, towards Swauk Pass and Wenatchee. Go 1 mile past Mineral Springs Campground and Restaurant.

Turn left onto Forest Service Rd. 9738. Turn left onto F.S. Rd. 9702 in 2 miles, towards Red Top. Hike the 1 mile round trip to the lookout tower.

Go back down to Rd. 9738, and turn left. Continue about 12 miles on Rd. 9738. Left at the T onto Teanaway River Rd. Right on E. Masterson Rd. Right on W. Masterson Rd. Right on Cle Elum Airport Rd. at the T. Right at the next T, and continue as the road bears to the left. Continue straight onto First St. Arrive back at First St. and Pennsylvania Ave.

Lion Rock Lookout and Liberty Townsite

65 Miles (25 gravel)
High Point: 6359'
2 1/2 hours driving time

This drive takes in an interesting geological sight and historical site. Lion Rock Lookout was perched on the edge of Table Mountain until 1967, when it was removed. Of course, the view is just as good now as it was then, it is just that the Forest Service has other ways of looking for forest fires. More impressive in a way is Table Mountain itself, which you travel on top of to get to the lookout. Table Mountain is a plateau above a columnar basalt cliff. The road is on top of the plateau, a fact you could overlook if you didn't take an opportunity to go over to the edge at one of the pullouts for an overlook. The cliff is also visible from the lookout.

Liberty was first inhabited in 1880 when gold was discovered. In 1891 one of the miners hit a big streak, and the twin towns of Liberty and Meaghersville really became going concerns. By 1916 the easy gold was gone, and the towns were nearly abandoned. The two little cities combined, choosing the name Liberty. Now, with new technology and the higher price of gold, interest in gold mining has been rekindled, and you'll see many active operations near town. In fact, you can try your luck at panning for gold while you're there. Liberty is a National Historic District, being the oldest mining townsite in the state, and you can take a look at the outdoor displays of old mining equipment and methods. The town has a handful of residents who have maintained the historic character of Liberty by building in the traditional style.

The Drive:

Head east on 1st St. in Cle Elum. Keep left at the I-90 interchange, continuing on Hwy. 970 towards Wenatchee. Keep left at the intersection with Hwy. 10, again continuing on Hwy. 970 towards Wenatchee. Straight at the junction with Hwy. 97, towards Swauk Pass and Wenatchee. Continue to the top of the pass.

Turn right at the top onto Forest Service Rd. 9716 towards Table Mountain. Left on F.S. Rd. 9712 in about 4 miles. Right on Rd. 35 in about 2 miles. Keep right at the fork in less than 1/2 mile. Continue 4 miles. Right on Rd. 124 towards Lion Rock Lookout and Lion Rock Campground (there is water available at the campground). Continue to the lookout site.

Return on Rd. 124. Left on Rd. 35, backtracking to Rd. 9712. Left on Rd. 9712, and continue about 8 miles to the town of Liberty. Left on the paved Liberty Rd. to the center of town. Stop in for some snacks and historical conversation at the grocery and gift store. Go back out on Liberty Rd. to Hwy. 97. Left on Hwy. 97. Continue into Cle Elum on Hwy. 97, then Hwy.970, reversing the way you came out.

Cross-Country Skiing

Traveling east of the mountains for a weekend of skiing, or just for a day, is worth the trip. Especially because the trip isn't really very long, and because it is a whole different world for skiing. It is usually colder and the snow is better because of it. And the sun

shines more often. Combined with the more open character of the forest and the wonderful play areas that provides, upper Kittitas County is a great place to cross-country ski.

The three routes in this book are reprinted with the kind permission of The Mountaineers Books and the authors. They are from *Cross-Country Ski Tours of Washington's South Cascades and Olympics* by Tom Kirkendall and Vicky Spring, published by The Mountaineers. We have selected a sampling of the basic skill level tours, to encourage beginners to give skiing a try. If you are an experienced skier, pull out your copy of *Cross-Country Ski Tours,* come on over the mountains and enjoy one of the more challenging routes.

You can also enjoy skiing from seven Sno-Park lots along I-90 in Upper Kittitas County. A $15 season parking pass opens miles of groomed ski trails. The Sno-Park lots with groomed ski trails are: Cabin Creek, at Exit 63, intermediate skiers go south 6.5 miles to Lake Easton, and advanced skiers go north 6.3 miles; Crystal Springs Rock, .5 mile south of Exit 62, 7 miles one-way for beginning skiers.

For more information about Sno-Park skiing, to buy a Sno-Park pass, or to buy a state-wide groomed cross-country ski trails map ($3.00), write to the Office of Winter Recreation, Washington State Parks and Recreation Commission, 7150 Cleanwater Lane, Olympia, Washington, 98504-5711, (206) 586-0185. Sno-Park passes are also available at over 125 retail locations throughout the state.

John Wayne Pioneer Trail

Skill level: basic   Best : January - February
Round trip: up to 15 miles   Avalanche potential: low
Skiing time: up to 7 hours   Maps: Green Trails, Cle Elum
Elevation loss: 120 feet
High point: 1840 feet

A ski tour across the state of Washington—now there's a thought to inspire the fantasy of skiers. Surprisingly, in the future such a dream could materialize along the old Milwaukee Road railroad grade.

When the Milwaukee Road was abandoned by the railroad, the section from Easton to the Idaho border was obtained for the state. It was named John Wayne Pioneer Trail by the hard-working group of equestrians who had the foresight to lobby the legislature before the land was taken over by private interests. The trail is dedicated to all non-motorized travel—skis and snowshoes in the winter and horses, hikers, and mountain bikers in the summer. The state is involved in working out the right of way along the old grade and so far has managed to place 25 miles under State Parks jurisdiction. The remainder of trail is currently under the control of the Department of Natural Resources (DNR) and open to public travel April 15 to May 31 and in October, not very handy for skiers. The DNR currently does not have the resources to maintain the rest of the trail, which is being taken over by adjoining property owners.

The trail starts in the town of Easton and heads through the rural Yakima River Valley, crossing the river twice on airy railroad bridges. The most isolated and scenic section of the trail is the last seven miles, which end at an old tunnel in a narrow, rock-walled gorge of the Yakima River.

Access:
Drive 22 miles east of Snoqualmie Pass on Interstate 90 to Exit 84 and drive .7 toward Cle Elum. As the road descends into town, turn right, following signs to Swiftwater Trailer Park. In the next .3 mile the road passes under the freeway, crosses the Yakima

River, enters South Cle Elum, and becomes Fourth Street. Bear left, uphill, .6 mile to an intersection and take a left on Lower Peoh Point Road. Drive 2.2 miles and pass under I-90 again. At .6 mile beyond the underpass find the trail access and parking on the left side of the road (1840 feet).

The Tour:

Ski down the steep embankment to the old railroad, then head east past a small barn and adjacent cows. On the left are the Yakima River and occasional glimpses of the Stuart Range. In 1 mile you'll see the ice-clad Teanaway and Yakima Rivers converging.

The trail tunnels through a grove of trees, then returns to the river, passing a broad swath of buzzing powerlines at 2 1/2 miles. Ahead the valley opens into Bristol Flat, an isolated section of level farmland boxed in by hills.

Continue straight ahead on flat terrain, passing a large overflow from an irrigation canal on the hill above. At 4 1/2 miles pass a couple of old shacks, remains of the old town of Horlick. The river now bends to the east as the valley narrows, and on the opposite side Highway 10 climbs above the level of the trail for the first time. The scenery becomes dramatic as the trail cuts through the steep canyon walls only a few feet above the sweeping torrent of the Yakima River.

The trail ends at 7 1/2 miles, in a shaded bend of the river where the winter sun rarely penetrates. Here railroad workers built a tunnel rather than blast a bench along the sheer canyon walls of basalt. turn around here— the section beyond requires a permit. Enjoy the scenery, but do so on day trips only - no camping allowed on the Duke's trail.

Teanaway River

Skill level: basic
Round trip: 4 miles or more
Skiing time: 2 hours or more   Avalanche Potential: low
Elevation loss: 100 feet   Maps: Green Trails
High point: 2500 feet
Best : January - March

Yes, the Teanaway River Road sees a lot of snowmobile traffic. Yes, the area has acquired a bad reputation among skiers. So do we recommend skiing here? Yes, yes, yes!

Despite the inconvenience of skiing among a gaggle of machines, midwinter skiing on the beautiful road bordering the Teanaway River can be a joy. You'll be treated to large scenic meadows, gently rolling terrain, and exhilarating views of the Stuart Range.

Access:

To reach the Teanaway River area drive 5 miles northeast from Interstate 90 on Highway 970, then turn left on Teanaway River Road. Following the "North Fork Teanaway," drive 9 miles to the end of the plowed road (2500 feet), or onward to the snowline, wherever that is.

Because this is a low-elevation trip, the snowline fluctuates wildly—especially in December. If you drive beyond the end of the plowed road, be sure to get out fast if snow starts falling. No plows will come to rescue you and your vehicle beyond the Lick Creek turnoff.

The Tour:

From the snowplow turnaround, ski up the road paralleling the North Fork Teanaway River. After 1 1/2 miles the road crosses the river, passes the Dickey Creek Campground, and heads through the first of a series of meadows. At 2 miles Mount Stuart and its satellites suddenly come into view. Take a good look, then continue on through the trees and more views for another 3/4 mile.

At 4 1/4 miles the road divides at 29 Pines Campground (2500feet). This makes a good turnaround point or overnight campsite. If you

drove this far without encountering snow, take the right fork and continue up the valley toward Esmerelda Basin, where the skiing should be good.

Swauk Pass Loops

Skill level: basic
Round trip: 1-5 miles
Skiing time: 3 hours - all day   Avalanche Potential: low
Elevation loss: up to 500 feet   Maps: Green Trails, Liberty
High point: 4400 feet
Best : January - February

Deep in the heart of snowmobile country the Forest Service has reserved an area around Swauk Pass for travelers powered solely by bread, cheese, and enthusiasm. Although this area is not large, it is crisscrossed with so many trails that you can ski for an entire day without covering them all.

This is undoubtedly the best-developed "no fee" area set aside for skiers in the entire Washington Cascades. The Forest Service and local ski clubs deserve considerable approbation for the project, which includes marking of trails and the placement of numerous trail maps.

Access:
Drive Highway 97 to Swauk Pass Summit (4102 feet), where Sno-Parks exist on both the north and south sides of the highway. Additional parking with access to the trails exists on the north side of the pass at .8 miles and 1.2 miles north of the summit.

The Tour:
The best tours for beginners are the Tronson Meadows loops. Park on the east side of the highway .8 mile below the pass and ski the logging roads to the Practice Meadow, located 1 1/2 miles from the highway. The meadows have a very gentle slope, just steep enough for beginners to practice. More advanced skiers will find challenge on the sections of trail connecting the roads. Side-Step Hill Trail

leads to two open meadows steep enough to carve a long string of turns. Near the Practice Meadow, Tronson Meadow Trail climbs up to meet the Haney Meadow Trail. This provides intermediate skiers with a loop to Swauk Pass and back.

Opposite the highway from Tronson Meadows is the lower access to 2 1/2 miles of trails on the north side of Swauk Pass. These loops start 1 mile below Swauk Pass at Tronson Campground. Park at the gated campground entrance and ski down into the snow-covered campsite loops. Beginners and snow players can make 1/2-mile loops through the camp area. Intermediate skiers will find a longer loop starting opposite the "Picnic Only" area.

Head uphill to an open slope and climb to the top. Take a skid road to the right and follow it to within 100 feet of the end. Climb uphill through a small basin and then up a rounded knoll to twisted trees and views to the Stuart Range. Ski left, back to the skid road, to complete the loop.

From the south-side Sno-Park at the summit of the pass, skiers can follow trails down to the Tronson Meadows area, ski the well-packed "shared corridor" (a logging road shared with snowmobiles), or take the challenging loop through Swauk Meadows. The loop though the meadows starts opposite the information board at the upper end of the Sno-Park. Ski across the top of the small snow-play area, then head steeply uphill on a old skid road. After 3/4 mile, the trail reaches the "shared corridor"; go right on the road for 1/4 mile to the top of a long open area. This is Swauk Meadows. Enjoy a long run down and at the bottom bear right into a second meadow. Follow blue diamonds into woods for an exhilarating run down a skid road. Then parallel the highway back to the Sno-Park.

The north-side Sno-Park serves as an alternate starting point for the ski loops originating at Tronson Campground. It also serves as a starting point for a "superloop" adventure which links the north-side trails to Tronson Meadows and Swauk Pass.

Snowmobiling

Upper Kittitas County is a great place for snowmobiling—one of the most popular in the state. The opportunities are almost endless, from attractive groomed routes, to lonely logging roads, to high country bowls. Go up high, cross an open meadow, and look out to the Stuart Range, across towards Ellensburg, or over to Mt. Rainier and the peaks of the Cascades. A few groomed routes are described here in detail, just for starters. The snow is usually good from the beginning of December though the end of April or early May.

Lake Cle Elum Ridge Riders is the local snowmobiling club. Its unofficial headquarters is the Last Resort - a restaurant and motel about 9 miles northwest of Cle Elum on Hwy. 903, on Cle Elum Lake. The Last Resort is snowmobile central for the Upper Kittitas Valley. If you're heading out, you should plan a stop to check on the current snow conditions, to get more suggestions on where to ride, or to just tell stories with other snowmobilers. You will find someone there from 7:00 am until at least 9:00 pm everyday. You are welcome to join the Lake Cle Elum Ridge Riders on their scheduled rides. Contact Margaret or Don for specific information: Margaret and Don May, The Last Resort, P.O. Box 532, Roslyn, WA 98941, (509)649-2222.

Watch for the annual YamaFest in mid-January at Cle Elum Lake. It is a weekend of fun for everyone, with day rides suited to every taste, a radar run to see who can really make their machine move, a big friendly tent for home base, a dance in the evening, and 3500 snowmobilers to enjoy it all.

Many routes in the Cle Elum Ranger District are groomed for snowmobiling. The Washington State Snowmobile Association

(WSSA) contracts with the National Forest Service and individuals to keep 235 miles of snowmobile routes groomed in Kittitas County. Pick up your Mountain View Gazette at the Cle Elum Ranger District Office; it includes an overview map and four detailed quadrant maps of snowmobile routes in the Cle Elum Ranger District. For even more, contact the Office of Winter Recreation, Washington State Parks and Recreation Commission, 7150 Cleanwater Lane, Olympia, Washington, 98504-5711, (206) 586-0185.

Swauk Pass

Of the miles and miles of groomed routes in Kittitas County, the area around Swauk Pass is one of the favorites. There are two routes described here, but the best way to plan your trip is to get one of the Winter Recreation Map and Brochures from the state (see the introduction to this section). For the Teanaway Loop you can also park on the Teanaway River Road, off of Hwy. 970, where you won't need a permit.

Lion Rock Lookout and Table Mountain
From the Sno-Park at Swauk Pass take Forest Service Rd. 9716 south towards Table Mountain. Left on F.S. Rd. 9712 in about 4 miles. Right on Rd. 35 in about 2 miles. Continue 4 miles. Right on Rd. 124 towards Lion Rock Lookout and Lion Rock Campground. Continue about 1/2 mile to the lookout site. Continue on Rd. 35 towards Reecer Creek until your gas is half gone, or your fingers are, and return the same way you came.

Loop to Teanaway Valley
From Mineral Springs, head up F.S. Rd. 9738. Continue about 15 miles, up the Teanaway Ridge and down along Jack Creek. Left on Teanaway Valley Road, and continue 2.5 miles. Left on Dickey Creek Rd. (if you reach the plowed lot, go back a bit over a mile and turn right on Dickey Creek Rd.). Continue on the groomed route onto Rd. 9702. Take the side trip up to Red Top Lookout, especially if it is a clear day. Continue down, turning right on Rd. 9738, and continue 2 miles to Mineral Springs.

Cooper River Road

The best thing about the Cooper River route isn't even on the route. It is up past the end of it. The groomed section leads up to the real attraction: a snowmobile playground in an open bowl. Get out and have fun! The trip up will take between 45 minutes and an hour, so plan a couple of hours for travel and extra time for playing.

Drive:

Take Hwy. 903 through Roslyn and Ronald, and along Cle Elum Lake. Park in the plowed lot on your left about 4 miles past the end of Cle Elum Lake at Forest Service Road 46.

Snowmobile:

Cross the bridge over the Cle Elum River, and continue to the end of the groomed route. Then play around before returning the same way.

Fish Lake Trail

This groomed route leads to a challenging and spectacular snowmobiling area off of the well-beaten path. It is simply called "Gallagher" by the local snowmobilers, and it is the area around Gallagher Head Lake. For a good snowmobile rider, one who can ride up and break through a cornice, the view to Mt. Rainier and the Cascade peaks is unbeatable. For someone who isn't quite ready for that kind of terrain, the area is only slightly less incredible. Getting into Gallagher is the most difficult of the snowmobile options in this guide. It takes about an hour and a quarter to get up to the end of the groomed route. It takes about two and a half hours to get into the Gallagher Head Lake area. Be sure you are prepared for a full day of snowmobiling when you head out.

Drive:

Take Hwy. 903 through Roslyn and Ronald, to the Salmon la Sac Picnic Area. Park in the plowed area at the end of the road.

Snowmobile:

The groomed route on Rd. 4330 goes about 10 miles to the end of the road at Fish Lake Campground (at Tucquala Lake). The real attraction of this route is the side trip to Gallagher Head Lake. The

route is not groomed from where you turn off and head up along Fortune Creek, but it is a popular destination, so the way may be broken by others already. Stop by at the Last Resort for information about whether anyone has been up since the last snow, and for detailed route instructions.

Motorcycling

Come out and enjoy trail riding in the Taneum - Manastash area. It is one of the most popular areas for trailbikes and short-wheelbase four wheel drives, and has eighty-seven miles of trailbike trails and twenty-six miles of four-wheel drive trails. There are routes for all skill levels, including many miles of trails with an Easy rating. Wind along in a heavily forested valley like Taneum Creek, or get up high to the open meadows and spectacular views on Quartz Mountain. Make a day trip from Cle Elum, or camp in one of the many free campgrounds in the area.

Stop at the Cle Elum Ranger District Office, west of the center of town on Second St. (also Hwy.903) for a packet of ORV maps of Eastern Washington. The maps, and the accompanying Washington Off-Road Vehicle Guide, are produced by the Washington State Department of Natural Resources (DNR). The Taneum-Manastash Area map in the packet is an indispensable guide to routes open to off-road vehicles, the difficulty of each route, exact mileages of each section of trail, and the topography of the area. The Guide outlines all of the ORV areas in the state and includes background information about off-roading, addresses of clubs and agencies involved in motorcycling, trail maintenance tips, and a bibliography of books and videos.

For your copy of the Off-Road Vehicle Guide and the Eastern and/or Western map packet, write: Interagency Committee for Outdoor Recreation, 4800 Capitol Boulevard KP-11, Tumwater, WA, 98504-5611. Or call (206) 753-7140.

Quartz Mountain

Miles: 43.2

High Point: 6100 feet

Quartz Mountain is a really terrific place. The view from the top, at 6100 feet, includes Mt. Adams, Mt. Rainier, peaks in the Alpine Lakes Wilderness, Mt. Stuart and the Stuart Range, the Goat Rocks, Lake Cle Elum and lots of wildflowers. Even though you have to do about half of this loop on dirt roads, it is worth it to get up to see this gigantic view. The way up travels through open meadows and finally into sub-alpine areas. The trip down is just plain fun, almost totally on trails. Most of the trails are designated "Easy" on the State ORV map, but there are 4.5 miles of "More Difficult" rated trail. Take plenty of food, water, and tools. You get pretty far from anything on this route!

Drive:
Start at First St. and Pennsylvania Ave. Go west on First St. Cross the railroad tracks. Left at the Y towards South Cle Elum. Continue across the Yakima River. This road becomes 4th St. in South Cle Elum. Right on Madison St. Left on 6th St. at the four way stop. Continue 2.5 miles; the road becomes Canyon Reservoir Rd. Turn left onto Forest Service Rd. 3350. You will see the sign to Peoh Point. Continue up for 6 miles. Park at the big intersection at the top (Five Corners).

The Ride:
Take Rd. 119 at the top (to the right as you approach the intersection). In just under 2 miles, turn left at the T onto Rd. 133. At mile 5.1 turn right towards Quartz Mountain on Rd. 3330. Stay on the main road; there are lots of logging and ORV routes branching off this road.

At a major intersection at mile 13.5 continue on Rd. 3120 (straight ahead) marked to Quartz Mt. (Tamrack Spring is 2 miles to the left, and Buck Meadow is 6 miles straight ahead.) Continue straight through another well-marked intersection showing Quartz Mt. 10 miles straight ahead, Ellensburg to the left 29 miles, and Buck Meadow 5 miles. Continue straight as a big road goes to the right

(mile 16).

At 17.5 turn right at the T where the sign reads Quartz Mt. 6 miles; Ellensburg 26 miles (in the other direction). Keep left at the intersection with Rd. 120 at mile 19.9, and continue up. Pass Quartz Spring Campground; tables, outhouse, no water. Continue up to the top of Quartz Mountain, reaching the top at mile 23.4.

Then come down just a tenth of a mile, and turn left onto the Manastash Ridge Trail. Or use the fork of the trail which you will find about 30 yards beyond the sign; it is less steep and rocky. The trail splits near the beginning; take either leg of the fork, they meet later on. In 1/2 mile after starting on the trail, keep right to join Trail 1363. Continue straight on Taneum Ridge Trail 1363.

Turn right at the edge of the clearcut at mile 26, and continue on the trail. When you come to the logging road in the clearcut, look for the trail directly on the other side and continue for 5.7 miles. Arrive at a wide trail intersection at mile 32. Turn left on Fishhook Flat Trail, 1378. Turn left on Rd. 3300 in a few yards, then right onto Fishhook Flat Trail in another few yards.

At mile 35.3, turn right at the T with the North Fork Taneum Trail 1377, towards Icewater Campground. Continue 5 miles. Turn left towards Cle Elum on Rd. 133, confirmed by the sign facing you reading Cle Elum to the left 13 miles; Taneum Campground to the right 5 miles. Arrive at Five Corners intersection at mile 43.2.

Taneum Trails

Miles: 19; 13 on trails, 6 on roads
High Point: 4000 feet

This loop, using trails for the most part, is just a sampling of the trails available in the Taneum area. The fun here is in trail riding, and since the route doesn't get up high, or into the open, views aren't the highlight. That makes this route a good choice on a cloudy day. If the weather is clear and beautiful, try to take the Quartz Mountain loop. If you don't have a State ORV map of the area, by all means, get one. It shows miles and miles of trails, most in the Easy and More Difficult categories, with a few miles with the Most Difficult designation. You can make many new loops of your own.

Drive:

Start at First St. and Pennsylvania Ave. Go west on First St. Cross the railroad tracks. Left at the Y towards South Cle Elum. Continue across the Yakima River. This road becomes 4th St. in South Cle Elum. Right on Madison St. Left on 6th St. at the four way stop. Continue 2.5 miles; the road becomes Canyon Reservoir Rd. Turn left onto Forest Service Rd. 3350. You will see the sign to Peoh Point. Continue up for 6 miles. Park at the big intersection at the top (Five Corners).

The Ride:

Take Rd. 111 (hard right as you arrived), and pass through an open gate. Don't take Rd. 119, the more traveled of the two. Left onto Rd. 113 in one mile. Left onto the trail as Rd. 113 begins to peter out. The trail is not marked, but it is well used on both sides of the road. Cross Rd. 119.

Right on paved Rd.33 at the bottom. Left at the Y to stay on Rd. 33, and cross a bridge. (There is an outhouse and informal camping near the intersection.) Watch for Taneum Ridge Trail (1363) on your right soon after crossing the bridge. Continue about 1.5 miles, come out on the road, turn right, and watch for the trail to continue on the right. Come out onto the road again at mile 8, again turning right.

Turn right onto Fishhook Flats Trail 1378 in just under half a mile. In 2.7 miles (mile 11.2), turn right on the North Fork Taneum Trail 1377, towards Icewater Campground. Continue 5 miles to Rd. 133. The sign facing you here points left to Cle Elum 13 miles, Taneum Campground is to the right 5 miles. Arrive at Five Corners intersection.

Fishing

Some people consider the Yakima River the best trout stream (excluding steelhead) in the entire state. The Yakima may produce some spectacular fish, but you're likely to have an equally pleasant and successful day at any one of a long list of less-famous spots. You can get away from I-90, up into the

mountains, and have wonderfully quiet day on a remote lake or stream - no one but you and the fish.

The information on fishing was reprinted from *Washington State Fishing Guide* by Stan Jones, Stan Jones Publishing. In the book, Mr. Jones includes information on forty-nine different lakes and streams in Upper Kittitas County. If you enjoy these spots, and would like a guide to others all over the state, get your own copy of the *Fishing Guide*. It is available in bookstores and sporting goods stores across Washington, or contact Stan Jones Publishing, 3421 E. Mercer St., Seattle, Washington, 98112; price: $9.95 post paid.

Yakima River

One of the best streams in the state for large trout, other than steelhead. Easily reached at countless points along the 90 miles from the lower end of Keechelus Lake to the city of Yakima. The upper river above Ellensburg produces rainbow, cutthroat, and eastern brook from May to October, depending upon water flow. Fall is prime fishing time. Below Ellensburg there are a few German browns in addition to the other species. The Yakima offers excellent whitefish angling in winter months. Top whitefish areas include the entire stretch from Cle Elum to Yakima County. Boat float trips through canyon stretches particularly in the fall are the most effective method of locating lunker trout. The lower canyon gets plants of rainbow from mid-May to late August, but wild fish are predominant. New access and boat launch areas have been built by the Dept. of Wildlife on the Roza pool, at the mouth of Umtanum Creek. Some restrictions—see official regs.

Cle Elum Lake

Enlarged by a dam of the natural lake on Cle Elum River, the lake covers 4810 acres and hosts rainbow, cutthroat, kokanee, Dolly Varden, eastern brook, whitefish, and fresh water ling cod. It comes on for 8-10 inch kokanee after June 1. An occasional mackinaw to 20 pounds is caught by trollers. Trolling is the most effective fishing method for most species in the lake. The big reservoir stretches for nearly 8 miles, and the road to Salmon la Sac touches it at a number of spots. Boats may be launched at Wish Poosh, and at Bell, Morgan, and Dry Creeks. Elevation of the lake is 2223 feet, and it is situated 7.3 miles N.E. of Cle Elum on the Salmon la Sac Road (Hwy. 903 in Cle Elum).

Swauk Creek

Follows Blewett Pass for about 15 miles and drains into the Yakima River. It is easily accessible and hosts rainbow, cutthroat, and a few eastern brook. Best fishing is early in the season. There are campsites and motels available.

Teanaway River

Enters Yakima River 1 mile E. of junction of Blewett Pass cut-off with I-90. A secondary road leaves the pass highway 3 miles from the junction and follows the river N.W. to Casland. The Teanaway splits into 3 forks here. Road up middle fork continues for 3 miles then trail takes off to headwaters near Jolly Mountain. Road up W. fork climbs over the ridge and drops to Cle Elum Lake. Road follows N. fork for 16 miles with branch roads offering access to tributaries including **Indian, Jack,** and **Stafford Creeks.** Other N. fork Tributaries are **Jungle, Beverly,** and **De Roux Creeks.**

 *Fishing*

The Teanaway is planted on a staggered basis through the season with rainbow and delivers best from June through August. By mid-August water levels are usually too low for good fishing. The stream is wadeable.

Cooper Lake

Eastern brook are the big attraction here but the 120 acre lake also has small kokanee. It lies at 2788 feet altitude 3 1/2 miles N.W. of Salmon la Sac. There are several campsites on the shores. To reach Cooper, turn left off Cle Elum River Road 1 mile S. of Salmon la Sac onto road 46. Boat launch facilities (non-motorized only). Prime fishing time is June, July, and October.

Fish Lake(Tucquala)

Popular lake of 63 acres located 7 1/2 miles N. of Salmon la Sac. It is a narrow, shallow, and weedy lake, and most fishing is done in channels. Fish Lake holds rainbow and eastern brook. Small boats may be launched adjacent to the road, where there are good camping spots. Meadows around the lake furnish good huckleberry picking in August and September.

Hansen's Ponds

A pair of rainbow-planted ponds situated at Cle Elum just S. of I-90. Public access. **Lavender Lake.** A 26-acre rainbow-stocked lake located 2 miles E. of Easton at East Nelson Siding interchange. **Lake Cle Elum.** A 25-acre lake located N. of I-90 at Cle Elum interchange. Stocked with rainbow. Pedestrian access only from old highway N. of lake..

Special Events

Taking part in or watching a special event is a great way to highlight a trip to Upper Kittitas County. Because things change, the events are just listed under the month, and you should call or write the Chamber of Commerce for more information about this year's date. Write: P.O. Box 43, Cle Elum, WA 98922; call (509) 674-5958; visit 221 E. First St., Cle Elum.

January
Wish Poosh Mush: Dog Sled Competition, Cle Elum Lake
Winter Carnival, Ronald and Cle Elum Lake
Winter Freight Race and Weight Pull: Dog Sleds, Iron Horse State Park in South Cle Elum
YamaFest: Snowmobile Fun Weekend, Cle Elum Lake

February
Snow Hopper Mountain Bike Race, Iron Horse State Park in Easton

May
Roslyn Riders Horse Play Day

June
Kayak Races, Salmon la Sac Guard Station

July
Pioneer Days, Cle Elum
Runner Stumbles 10K Run, Roslyn
Men's Softball Tournament, Cle Elum
Washington Old-Time Fiddlers Workshop, Cle Elum
Coal Bowl Women's Softball Tournament, Cle Elum

August
Run to Roslyn Custom Car Show, Roslyn
Roslyn Wing Ding Community Festival, Roslyn

September
Ellensburg Rodeo and Kittitas County Fair, Labor Day Week-

end, Ellensburg
Rock Hound Pow-Wow, Dickey Creek Campground

December
Christmas in Cle Elum, Cle Elum

Lodging

Each of these establishments is a member of the Cascade Lodging Association, which assures small town hospitality, comfort, and cleanliness.

Bonita Motel
906 E. First St., Cle Elum 98922
(509) 674-2380
Dick and Lorraine Lago, owners
Nine rooms, one with kitchen; cable TV. RV park with 11 sites. Across from 24 hour restaurant.

Cedars Motel
1001 E. First St., Cle Elum 98922
(509) 674-5535
Gene and Janie Westlund, owners
The Cedars Motel offers a clean, courteous atmosphere to enhance your relaxation. AAA rating, 24 hour restaurant.

Chalet Motel
800 E. First St., Cle Elum 98922
(509) 674-2320
Joe and Kathy Thomas, owners
Eleven meticulously cleaned rooms with cable TV. Free airport shuttle for our guests.

Coal Country Inn
46 N. Second St., Roslyn 98941
(509) 649-3369
Maria and Jason Greenlee, owners
Come to Coal Country Inn of Roslyn and experience the natural beauty and rich history of the Cascades. We offer old

fashioned comforts, like oatmeal cookies and porch swings, in a rustic setting that reflects Roslyn's coal mining days.

Hidden Valley Guest Ranch
HC 61 Box 2060, Cle Elum 98922
(509) 857-2344
Bruce and Kim Coe, Matt Coe, owners
Eastern Washington's oldest and finest, nestled in a serene valley. Heated pool and hot tub, recreation lounge, horse and wagon rides and nature quests on our 750 acre ranch. Food and lodging packages.

The Last Resort
Hwy. 903, Cle Elum Lake 98940
(509) 649-2222
Don and Margaret May, owners
A warm, cozy motel complete with a family style restaurant and a service bar. One unit with kitchen; mini mart, storage units, RV hookups, and propane service.

MaMa Vallone
302 W. First St., Cle Elum 98922
(509) 674-5174
Dennis and Lexi Vallone, Joe Vallone, owners
The 2-story inn was built in 1904. It was originally a boarding house for teachers who taught the miner's children. Bed and breakfast rooms upstairs and a dining adventure downstairs.

Moore House Country Bed and Breakfast Inn
P.O. Box 2861, South Cle Elum 98943
(509) 674-5939
Connie and Monty Moore, owners
Come play through the seasons at our 11 room historic railway inn. Awake to the smell of fresh coffee and eggs benedict or blueberry pancakes.

Mt. Rose Lodge
Hwy. 903 and Pine Drive, Cle Elum Lake 98940
(509) 649-3409
A six bedroom lodge with full service restaurant and hot tub. Corporate retreats, hay & sleigh rides, guided snowmobile

trips, and historical tours.

Stewart Lodge
805 W. First St., Cle Elum 98922
(509) 674-4548
Bob and Patty Stewart, owners
A country motif sets the style for this brand new 24-unit motel, including a handicap unit. Unique pine furniture, cable TV,hot tub and swimming pool.

Timber Lodge
301 W. First St., Cle Elum 98922
(509) 674-5966
Tom and Jami McKnight, owners
Brand new Three Diamond AAA destination lodge and restaurant in the heart of Cle Elum. Spa, cable TV.

Restaurants

This is a list of restaurants in Upper Kittitas County in no order other than alphabetical. You'll find a wide variety of eating experiences, from drive-ins to fine dining.

Cavallini's
A nice little restaurant in the mountains.
200 E. First St., Cle Elum
674-2151

Cle Elum Bakery
Original brick oven, since 1906.
501 E. First St., Cle Elum
674-2233

The Cottage Cafe
Good ole American country food - open 24 hours.
911 E. First St., Cle Elum
674-2922

Cruise Inn
Home of the Warrior Burger. Best buy in town.
Hwy. 903, Roslyn
649-2318

Homestead Bar B-Q
Specializing in barbecue beef and pork ribs. Beer and wine available. 11:00am - 9:00pm 7 days a week.
East end of Cle Elum near exit 87 from I-90.
674-5174

The Last Resort
Hearty home-cooked meals; cocktails; homemade pies, soups, and salads.
Hwy. 903, Cle Elum Lake
649-2222

MaMa Valone's
Fine Italian cuisine; excellent service; old world charm and hospitality.
302 W. First St, Cle Elum
674-5174

The Matterhorn
Authentic German dishes; cocktails.
212 W. Railroad St., Cle Elum
674-2210

The Miner's Cafe
Breakfast, lunch, and dinner; salad bar daily.
Hours 7:00am - 9:00pm daily.
N. First St., Roslyn
649-2763

Pennsylvania Station
Cafe, deli, breakfast anytime. Old fashioned ice cream parlor.
#4 Pennsylvania Ave., Roslyn
649-2763

Roslyn Cafe
An oasis in historic downtown Roslyn.

2nd and Pennsylvania Ave., Roslyn
649-2763

Roslyn's Village Pizza
We deliver. Listed in "Northwest Best Places".
Open 4:30pm daily.
#6 Pennsylvania, Roslyn
649-2992

The Skookum Inn
Pleasant, quality dining at beautiful, friendly Cle Elum Lake.
Hwy. 903 and Pine Drive, Cle Elum Lake
674-3409

El Caporal III
Good meals, family mexican
107 W. 1st St., Cle Elum

The Sunset Cafe
Home of the coal car salad bar; specializing in Italian food.
318 E. First St., Cle Elum
674-5800

The Timberlodge Restaurant
Where tasteful homecooked food is served in the mountains.
310 W. First St., Cle Elum
674-5590

Camps, Outfitters, and Ranches

Camp Wahoo Youth Camp
A wilderness horse camp for boys and girls, ages 9 - 16.
Weekly sessions emphasizing horses, trail riding, outdoor
living skills, and wildlife.
(206) 392-0111

Flying Horseshoe Youth Camp
For boys and girls ages 7 - 15: horseback riding, outdoor

arena, daily trail riding. Two-week sessions at the oldest family-run youth camp in the state.
(509) 674-2366

3 Queens Outfitter and Guide Service
Day rides, pack trips, hunting, fishing, backpacking, drop camps, and photography.
(509) 674-6547

High Country Outfitters
Specializing in horses: guided day rides, overnights, extended deluxe pack trips, summer drop camps, cattle roundup, horse drive, and other programs.
(206) 392-0111

Hidden Valley Guest Ranch
Full overnight and dining accommodations. Horseback riding, hay rides, and groomed cross-country ski routes without snowmobiles.
(509) 674-5990

Outdoor Equipment Rentals, Sales, and Service

Cross-Country Skis
T&C Rental, Cle Elum	(509) 674-2877
Mountainholm, Easton	(509) 656-2346

Snowmobiles
Pioneer Rentals, Easton	(509) 656-2302
Sportland Yamaha, Roslyn	(509) 649-2259
Last Resort, Roslyn	(509) 649-2222

Mountain Bikes & Service
Mathes and Son, Roslyn	(509) 649-3423
Mountainholm, Easton	(509) 656-2346

River Rafts
River Raft Rentals, Ellensburg	(509) 964-2145

Wenatchee National Forest Campgrounds in Cle Elum Ranger District

Upper County Area

Cle Elum River ($4.00 per night)
Location: On the Cle Elum Valley Road #903, 15 miles north of Cle Elum.
Facilities: Pit toilets, tables, stoves.
Sites: 35 - camping or picnicking.
Activities: Tent and trailer camping, picnicking, fishing, hunting, hiking, group camping.

Owhi
Location: 5 miles off the Cle Elum Valley Road above Lake Cle Elum at Cooper Lake. turnoff is approximately 18 miles from Cle Elum Road #46. **Bridge out. No access until 1992.**
Facilities: Pit toilets, stoves, tables, parking lot, boat launch.
Sites: 23 walk-in camping or picnicking only; camper/trailer facilities not available.
Activities: Camping, picnicking, fishing, hiking, photography, non-motorized boating.

Crystal Springs ($4.00 per night)
Location: Adjacent to Interstate 90, 20 miles west of Cle Elum. **Closed until further notice. Check with Cle Elum Ranger Station.**
Facilities: Community kitchen, pit toilets, tables, stoves, piped water.
Sites: 20 camping, 10 picnicking.
Activities: Tent and trailer camping, picnicking, fishing, berry picking, mushrooming.

Fish Lake (Tucquala Lake)

Location: Fish Lake campground is located near Tucquala Lake approximately 29 miles from Cle Elum on the Cle Elum Valley Road. The road is paved to Salmon la Sac, 19 miles north of Cle Elum. The road beyond is narrow and rough and is not recommended for trailers.

Facilities: Pit toilets, tables, stoves, guard station.

Sites: 15 - camping or picnicking.

Activities: Camping, picnicking, fishing, hunting, hiking, photography, berry picking.

Kachess ($6.00 per night)

Location: On Lake Kachess, approximately 5 miles off Interstate 90. The campground is about 27 miles from Cle Elum and 65 miles from Seattle. Access is by paved road #49.

Facilities: Flush and pit toilets, piped water,tables, stoves, 1 primary boat launch and 1 unimproved boat launch, swimming area, self-guided interpretive trail, guard station.

Sites: 180 camping, (42 reservation units); 30 picnicking; one group unit (45 persons).

Activities: Tent and trailer camping, picnicking, fishing, hiking, swimming and wading, photography, waterskiing, boating, berry picking.

Red Mountain

Location: On the Cle Elum Valley Road #903, 16 miles north of Cle Elum.

Facilities: Pit toilets, stoves, tables.

Sites: 12 - camping or picnicking.

Activities: Tent camping, picnicking, fishing, hiking.

Salmon la Sac ($6.00)

Cayuse Horse Camp ($4.00 per night)

Location: At the end of the Cle Elum Valley Road #903, 25 miles north of Cle Elum.

Facilities: Piped water, flush toilets, community kitchen, stoves, tables, guard station, 15-unit horse camp, public corrals, loading ramp.

Sites: 127 camping, (26 reservation units); 50 picnicking;
             8 double family, 1 group reservation site (100
             persons).
Activities: Tent and trailer camping, picnicking, fishing hunt-
             ing, hiking, horseback riding.

Wish Poosh ($6.00 per night)
Location: 8 miles northwest of Cle Elum, on the Cle Elum
             Valley Road #903.
Facilities: Single and double family camp units, picnicking
             units, flush toilets, piped water, barbecue grills,
             paved boat launch, swimming beach, parking lot.
Sites: 39 camping; 16 picnicking.
Activities: Tent and trailer camping, picnicking, fishing, swim-
             ming, boating, water-skiing.

Swauk - Table Mountain Area

Lion Rock Spring
Location: On Road #35, 23 miles north of Ellensburg.
Facilities: Pit toilet, tables, benches, fire rings, water (live
             stock only).
Sites: 3 - camping or picnicking.
Activities: Viewing scenery, camping, picnicking, hunting,
             hiking, horseback riding, motorcycle riding - all
             available on or near site.

Mineral Springs ($4.00 per night)
Location: On U.S. Highway 97, 21 miles east of Cle Elum.
Facilities: Pit toilets, tables, stoves, fire rings, piped water,
             nearby restaurant/lounge.
Sites: 12 - camping or picnicking.
Activities: Camping, picnicking, fishing, hunting; rock
             hounding within 5 miles.

Red Top
Location: End of Road #9702, near Red Top Lookout, 28
             miles east of Cle Elum.
Facilities: Pit toilets, tables, fire grills, parking lot for 20 cars,
             fire lookout.

Sites: 3 - camping or picnicking.
Activities: Rockhounding, camping, picnicking, hiking, viewing scenery, hunting.

Swauk ($5.00 per night)
Location: On U.S. Highway 97, 27 miles east of Cle Elum.
Facilities: Comfort station, vault toilets, community kitchen, tables, stoves, fire rings, piped water, horseshoe pits, swings, trail, baseball backstop.
Sites: 23 camping, 22 picnicking.
Activities: Camping, picnicking, group sports, group picnics, viewing scenery, hiking, hunting, fishing.

Teanaway Area

Beverly
Location: On North Fork Teanaway Road #9737, 25 miles north of Cle Elum.
Facilities: Vault toilets, tables, fire grills.
Sites: 16 - camping or picnicking.
Activities: Camping, picnicking, fishing, hunting, hiking, horseback riding, motorcycle riding.

Taneum - Manastash Area

Buck Meadows
Location: On Road #31, 24 miles west of Ellensburg.
Facilities: Pit toilet, tables, fire rings.
Sites: 5 - camping or picnicking.
Activities: Camping, picnicking, viewing scenery, hunting, hiking, horseback riding, motorcycle riding.

Tamarack Spring
Location: On Road #3120 at forest boundary, 25 miles south of Cle Elum.
Facilities: Pit toilet, table, water (livestock only).
Sites: 2 - camping or picnicking.
Activities: Camping, picnicking, hunting, hiking, horseback riding, motorcycle riding.

Taneum ($4.00 per night)
Location: On Taneum Road #33, 18 miles south of Cle Elum.
Facilities: Vault toilets, tables, stoves or fire rings, community
            kitchen, piped water.
Sites: 13 camping; 16 picnicking.
Activities: Camping, picnicking, fishing, hunting, hiking,
            horseback riding, motorcycle riding.

Icewater Creek
Location: On Taneum Road #33, 20 miles south of Cle
            Elum.
Facilities: Vault toilets, tables, stoves, water, motorcycle
            practice trail.
Sites: 17 camping and 3 picnicking.
Activities: Camping, picnicking, fishing, hunting, hiking,
            horseback riding, motorcycle riding.

Haney Meadows
Location: Off U.S. 97, on Road #9722, 40 miles east of Cle
            Elum.
Facilities: Tables, stoves, vault toilets, council area, horse
            tethering, loading facilities.
Sites: 18 single family, 17 multiple family sites.
Activities: Camping, picnicking, hunting, hiking, horseback
            riding.

State Park

Lake Easton State Park
Location: 1 mile west of Easton on I-90.
Facilities: Tables, stoves, boat launch, trailer dump, facilities
            for disabled.
Sites: 91 camping, 45 hookup sites with water, electricity
            & sewer, 2 primitive sites.
Activities: Camping, picnicking, swimming, fishing cross coun-
            try skiing, snowmobiling, winter play.

Private Campgrounds and RV Parks (all area code 509)

Call these campgrounds for more information about their facilities and reservations.

Lake Easton Resort, Easton	656-2255
Eagle Valley, Cle Elum	674-7762
RV Town, Easton	656-2360
Sun Country Golf Resort	674-2226
Trailer Corral, Cle Elum	674-2433
Mineral Springs Resort, Mineral Springs	857-2310
Bonita RV Park	674-2380

Notes

Notes

Notes